# TRADITIONS AND CELEBRATIONS

# CHINESE NEW YEAR

T0025417

by Sharon Katz Cooper

PEBBLE
a capstone imprint

Pebble Explore is published by Pebble, an imprint of Capstone.
1710 Roe Crest Drive
North Mankato, Minnesota 56003
www.capstonepub.com

**Library of Congress Cataloging-in-Publication Data**
Names: Katz Cooper, Sharon, author.
Title: Chinese New Year / by Sharon Katz Cooper.
Description: North Mankato, Minnesota : Pebble, 2021. | Series: Pebble explore. Traditions and celebrations | Includes bibliographical references and index. | Audience: Ages 6-8 | Audience: Grades 2-3 |
Summary: "Chinese New Year is a time for new beginnings. Some people clean their homes from top to bottom or share meals with friends. Others pray, light fireworks, or give each other gifts. Readers will discover how a shared holiday can have multiple traditions and be celebrated in all sorts of ways"-- Provided by publisher.
Identifiers: LCCN 2020037997 (print) | LCCN 2020037998 (ebook) | ISBN 9781977131843 (hardcover) | ISBN 9781977132864 (paperback) | ISBN 9781977153999 (pdf) | ISBN 9781977155702 (kindle edition) Subjects: LCSH: Chinese New Year--Juvenile literature. | China--Social life and customs--Juvenile literature. Classification: LCC GT4905 .K385 2021 (print) | LCC GT4905 (ebook) | DDC 394.261--dc23 LC record available at https://lccn.loc.gov/2020037997 LC ebook record available at https://lccn.loc.gov/2020037998

**Image Credits**
Dreamstime: Arne9001, 25, Wei Wei, 20; Getty Images: China Photos/Stringer, 16, ED JONES/Staff, 8, SOPA Images/Contributor, 17; iStockphoto: faidzzainal, 14, Image Source, 7, real444, 21; Shutterstock: 123Nelson 19, atiger, 11, Boontoom Sea-Kor, 15 (right), ChameleonsEye, 18, Fotokostic, 22, Gayvoronskaya_Yana, 27, glen photo, 26, Igor Kardasov, 23, Jarvna, 15 (left), knyazev vasily, cover, 1, Lukas Kirka, 10, Mariusz S. Jurgielewicz, 29, Saigoneer, 5, Toa55, 9, Wakllaff, 13, Winston Tan, 28, wong sze yuen, 4, 24

Artistic elements: Shutterstock/Rafal Kulik

**Editorial Credits**
Editor: Jill Kalz; Designer: Juliette Peters; Media Researcher: Kelly Garvin; Production Specialist: Spencer Rosio

**Consultant Credits**
Lea Walker, Director
Chinese Culture Center
Columbia, South Carolina

All internet sites appearing in back matter were available and accurate when this book was sent to press.

# TABLE OF CONTENTS

Words in **bold** are in the glossary.

# WHAT IS CHINESE NEW YEAR?

Chinese New Year is a special time. It marks the start of a new year. It is the most important holiday in China. People have **celebrated** it for more than 2,000 years!

Chinese New Year is also called the Lunar Calendar New Year or the Spring Festival. It happens between the middle of January and the middle of February. The holiday starts on the first new moon of the first month of the **lunar calendar**. It lasts 15 days.

People around the world celebrate Chinese New Year. The largest gatherings are in China, Hong Kong, and Taiwan.

Many people share the same holiday **traditions**. Cleaning is one of them. People clean their homes to get rid of bad luck and make room for good luck. They hang **lanterns**. They put short poems and art on the walls. People hope these things will bring good luck in the new year.

# SPECIAL DAYS

There are two extra-special days during Chinese New Year. The fifth day is the Festival of Po Wu. It welcomes the god of **wealth**. On this day, some shop owners set off firecrackers. They hope it will bring money in the new year.

The 15th day is the Festival of Lanterns. People hang all kinds of paper lanterns. They may write riddles on them. It is a colorful way to end the holiday.

# ANIMAL OF THE YEAR

Every year on the Chinese lunar calendar gets its own animal. The animals are rat, ox, tiger, rabbit, dragon, snake, horse, goat, monkey, rooster, dog, and pig. Every 12 years, the animals repeat.

**Chinese lunar calendar**

The new year's animal is on many decorations. For example, 2020 was the year of the rat. Wall hangings, lanterns, and cards had pictures of rats on them. The ox gets its turn in 2021. The tiger is the animal for 2022.

# LET'S EAT!

Food is a big part of Chinese New Year. Some people believe certain foods can make wishes come true.

They say eating sweets will bring good things. Eating **dumplings** may bring money. If someone wants a baby, they are told to eat fruits with lots of seeds. What if you want more of everything? Some people say to eat fish.

Dinner on Chinese New Year's Eve is a feast. It often has eight parts. Many people eat at home. Others go to a restaurant. For most families, the dinner is a **reunion**.

**Eight Treasures Rice**

**Tang Yuan**

Rice dishes are very common. Eight Treasures Rice is rice with nuts, red beans, and dried fruit. Tang Yuan is a dessert soup with rice balls. Song Gao is a round sweet cake made from ground rice. Steamed fish is a New Year favorite for many people.

The big meal is only the start of the fun. Everyone tries to stay up all night on New Year's Eve. They talk, laugh, and eat more food.

People put red candles in all corners of the house. Many people also light fireworks. They believe the fireworks scare away evil spirits.

# OTHER TRADITIONS

Food is an important tradition for Chinese New Year. But it's not the only one! Dragons are another tradition. They are a sign of good luck in China. They are found in many New Year celebrations.

Dragon dances fill the streets. They get everyone moving! Drummers beat loudly on their drums. Dancers hold poles that move parts of a large dragon. The dragon twists and turns. It wiggles and waves. A long dragon body means lots of luck for the new year.

Many people wear red clothes for Chinese New Year. In China, red stands for good luck. It also stands for happiness. Red **banners** hang in many homes for the holiday.

People often give gifts. Older people give red envelopes to children. The envelopes hold money. Friends share food. They bring cakes, chocolates, and other sweets to one another's homes.

Some gifts should not be given for Chinese New Year. Clocks and watches are not good New Year gifts. They show that time is short.

You should not give sharp things, such as knives. They might cut your luck. This is also why many people do not get haircuts during the holiday. It's bad luck.

Chinese New Year is a time for people to gather. Family members of all ages have fun. Some families take a group photo every year. They wear red clothes. They may pose the same way each year.

**A family poses in a traditional New Year's greeting gesture.**

During the holiday, people may greet each other in a special way. Some say, "May all your wishes be fulfilled." Others say, "May your happiness be without limit."

Outdoor markets pop up in many cities at this time of the year. They sell goods that help people celebrate. There are firecrackers and special holiday foods. There are clothes and lots of fresh flowers.

kumquats

Flowers are a New Year tradition. Plum blossoms are said to bring good luck. Sunflowers bring a good year. Some fruits have meaning too. Apples are thought to keep sickness away. **Kumquats** bring wealth.

# IN THE UNITED STATES

People celebrate Chinese New Year around the world. In the United States, New York City has a week-long event. It includes a large party and concerts. Fireworks light up the sky over the Hudson River. There is also a parade.

San Francisco, California, has a parade too. More than 500,000 people celebrate the New Year there. Millions more watch on TV. Maybe you'll be one of them next year. Wear red and join the fun!

# GLOSSARY

**banner** (BA-nuhr)—a long piece of material with writing, pictures, or designs on it

**celebrate** (SEL-uh-brayt)—to do something fun on a special day

**dumpling** (DUMP-ling)—a piece of dough wrapped around a filling

**kumquat** (KUM-kwat)—a small, orangelike fruit

**lantern** (LAN-turn)—a light bulb or candle inside a frame that can be carried or hung

**lunar calendar** (LOO-nur KAL-uhn-dur)—calendar based on cycles of the moon

**reunion** (ree-YOON-yuhn)—a gathering of people who haven't seen each other in a long time

**tradition** (tra-DIH-shuhn)—a custom, idea, or belief passed down through time

**wealth** (WELTH)—lots of money

# HOW TO SAY IT

Festival of Po Wu (FES-tuh-vuhl UHV POH WOO)

Song Gao (SONG GOW)

Tang Yuan (TANG yoo-AHN)

# READ MORE

Amstutz, Lisa J. *Chinese New Year*. North Mankato, MN: Capstone Press, 2017.

Grack, Rachel. *Chinese New Year*. Minneapolis: Bellwether Media, Inc., 2017.

Murray, Julie. *Chinese New Year*. Minneapolis:

Abdo Kids Junior, 2019.

# INTERNET SITES

*Chinese New Year: All About the Holidays*
pbslearningmedia.org/resource/68938b4e-1e68-4727-8f2d-cc341ed93b11/chinese-new-year-all-about-the-holidays/

*Chinese New Year: Interesting Facts for Kids*
kids-world-travel-guide.com/chinese-new-year.html

*Crafts and Activities for Chinese New Year*
enchantedlearning.com/crafts/chinesenewyear/

# INDEX